GUITAR
APOPHENIA

A visualization study

Ric Criste

2014

Cover art by John Evanko

Over the course of years of teaching a repetition of guitarist's methods, I began to look for a different approach to learning the guitar. Going back to the basics of my learning was the key to what has evolved here.

We learn in pictures. You are much more likely to remember what you read *if you visualize it*. Putting yourself at "the scene" of a novel makes you visualize it, like your mind's movie.

The process of " Apophenia" or matrixing is giving form to things.
This is seeing meaningful patterns or connections in random data. When your eyes scan a crowd of people, you are looking for a familiar face that stands out. Your brain does this very rapidly. A face is a familiar shape.

This method breaks down the task of learning the guitar into "little pictures." It is easier to learn in parts, rather than digest the large pieces of the puzzle. This is not intended to be an all inclusive, comprehensive method. This method is meant to open doors and spark your own creativity. My intention also is to show you ways to aid you in improvisation, comping, memory retention, and also song writing.

There are two divisions in this method. Notated areas may be studied gradually, while the other sections must be completed before moving on. It is important that you grasp each concept presented here, before you move on. If you are able to teach another person each section you learn, you will have achieved that knowledge.

It is so important to write down personal ideas about the text that you may possibly forget. Write as if you won't see it again for a year, so you will understand what you meant when you reread it.

If you feel that you may know a particular section before reading it, please look at it also. This book is a <u>visual</u> approach. You may find you prefer teaching this way.

The Guitar Fretboard

Learning all the notes of the fretboard is a major task. Most people have learned the notes by counting up the musical alphabet, starting from the open string note. <u>My goal is to make everything easier!</u>

Try it this way using only three shapes:

(These are octave shapes. "Octo"= Eight). These are all G's.

Shape #1: *"One" string between notes, one fret in between.*

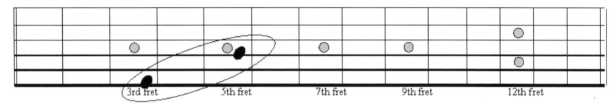

Shape #2: *"Two" strings in between the notes, one fret in between.*

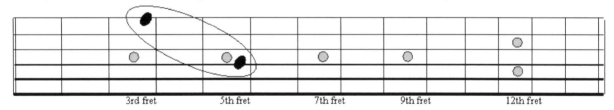

Shape #3: *"Three" frets above with one string in between.*

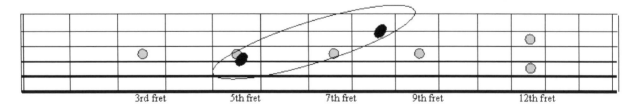

Notice how the shape <u>name</u> matches the shape. This makes it easy to remember. This is <u>Apophenia, giving form to things</u>. **These shapes are very important!**

Putting it all together:

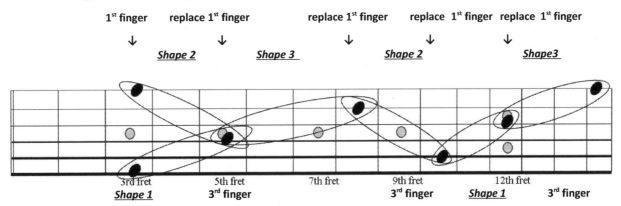

When changing positions, take care not to lose the position of the previous note. *Your first finger should start every new position.*

Everything repeats at 15th fret.

Overlaying shape #3 on 1st string 3rd fret will give you open G on the 3rd string.

These shapes are moveable up and down the neck. If we start on the 5th string and repeat the pattern, shape #2 doesn't work as before. We run out of strings. So skip to the next shape. All C's:

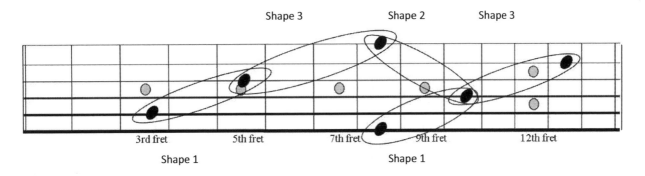

Thus the rule: Using shapes from the fifth string:

If you run out of strings, skip to the next shape. In some cases you may find yourself working backwards in shapes in order to cover all the notes. Use the same fingerings as previous exercise.

Additional shape—not needed at this point in study is **Shape #4**. I see this as *two strings between, two frets between.* *2+2=4*. This shape only works on the 6th string. These are octave A's.

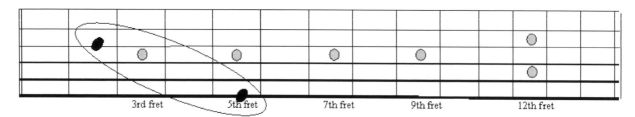

Be certain that your guitar is in tune when practicing this and ALL exercises. Your ear should tell you if you are out of tune.

Overview:

Being that you always have the reference pitch to start from, you should see and recognize the shapes very quickly. These two patterns work on any notes on the 5th and 6th strings. This will save you a very considerable amount of time learning the notes.

Playing through a sequence of all the G notes on the neck will hopefully take you less than 20 seconds. That is very little time. If you play through this sequence fifty times a day, (about fifteen minutes), you will start to remember the notes. Pick a different note each day to practice. When you're able to play these well, set your metronome to 60 and play the note of the day two places on each string, on each click of the metronome.

Do not move on until you understand *this concept*. The memorization of notes will come with use.

Gradual Study -Harmony

We need to look at some harmony here. Since we are playing music, it is necessary to learn the formula of music. Songs are not random chords, but follow a mathematical formula. However you don't have to be a math whiz to understand this.

If a song is in the key of *C major,* first we look at a C major scale:

C D E F G A B C

1 2 3 4 5 6 7 8

We will now harmonize the scale with chords. Chords are formed in thirds; from C to E is a 3rd. F to A is a 3rd also. It takes at least 3 notes to make a chord, the 1st note (or the root), the 3rd, and the 5th. The 5th is a 3rd above the 3rd.

   C   E   G   **← This is a *C* chord**

   1   3   5

Basically, we take the root of the chord (C), skip a note (D), take the next note or the third (E), skip a note (F), and take the next note or the fifth (G). This will form a C chord. This is called a *triad*- a three note chord.

"Tri" means three.

We need to study this. We spend much of our playing time using chords. You will soon see other ways this is useful.

Gradual Study

Let's Harmonize the Whole Scale:

C D E F G A B C D E F G A B C

1 2 3 4 5 6 7

This is two octaves (octo = eight, eight tones in the scale). This makes it easier to see.

C	--	CEG	C major	(C)	I
D	--	DFA	D minor	(Dm)	ii
E	--	EGB	E minor	(Em)	iii
F	--	FAC	F major	(F)	IV
G	--	GBD	G major	(G)	V
A	--	ACE	A minor	(Am)	vi
B	--	BDF	B diminished	(B°)	vii°

The major chords *C, F,* and *G* are the 1st, 4th, and 5th chords. They are major chords and are indicated by upper-case Roman Numerals; the other chords are indicated by the lower-case Roman Numerals. We will soon look at these chords more closely. If you play through these chords, they sound musically pleasing. If you play them instead, as all major chords, (*C major, D major, E major,* etc.) the result is not musically stable.

Gradual Study

As a songwriter, you can alter this formula somewhat, but you must take care. Use your ear as a guide; the formula we have discussed is the same in every major key. The sharps and flats in the other keys tend to make the less musically inclined person grind to a halt.

The circle or cycle of fifths is usually shown as a circle with letters around it mentioning 5[ths] and 4[ths]. You may need to have a more visual representation to "see" if you don't understand already.

We start with a C major scale. There are no sharps or flats in *C* because we don't need them. If you play C D E F G A B C, you will see that there is a half step (one fret), between E and F, and B and C. This is necessary to sound like a major scale (Do Re Mi Fa Sol La Ti Do). These half steps are naturally occurring. There are no notes between E and F or B and C.

A sharp raises a pitch by a half step, or one fret. (Between C and D is C#. C# is a higher pitch than C by a half step, or one fret).

Gradual Study

In a major scale, the half steps (one fret on the guitar) occur between the 3rd and 4th, and the 7th and 8th scale tones/degrees. The others are whole steps (two frets on the guitar). <u>The half steps have to be where they are</u>.

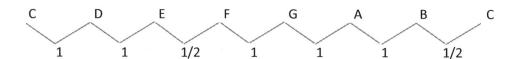

The circle of fifths is the progressive order of keys. The sharps and flats "correct" the half steps from being in the wrong place in the scale. The circle of fifths goes up in fifths. Our first key was *C*. The 5th above *C* is G.

C	D	E	F	G
1	2	3	4	5

(Think of a 5th as a power chord shape...a power chord is a chord composed of two notes, the root and its fifth, or C5 as it is written.)

So we prepare a *G* scale:

G	A	B	C	D	E	F	G
1	2	3	4	5	6	7	8

Remember the half steps at 3 & 4 and 7 & 8? B to C is a half step. F to G is not, so we sharp (♯), or raise, the F to F♯. This "fixes" the half step between 7 & 8. This also fixes 6 & 7 because between E and F is only a half step. When we add the sharp to F it creates a whole step between E and F, matching the formula.

Sharps

G major:

(We have corrected the scale with F#.)

G   A   B   C   D   E   F#   G

1/2   1   1/2

The hard part is over. Keep in mind we are counting in 5^{ths}. The 5th above *G* is the next key: *D major*

G A B C D

1 2 3 4 5

Write:

D   E   F   G   A   B   C   D   We will now add sharps.

From here on, through all the sharp keys, simply keep the sharps from the previous key (ex. G major = one sharp, **F#**) and <u>**sharp the 7th in the new key.**</u>

D   E   F#G   A   B   C# D

Kept from key before   Added

One more: A major

A B C# D E F# G# A

C# and F# have been kept from previous key (D). G# is added.

Note: The last sharp in a major scale is a half step below the key.

All Sharp Keys

Let's look at the whole circle sequence:

Use this for your reference until you memorize them all. As a guitar player, you should concentrate on the keys of *C, G, D, A,* and *E* first. These are popular guitar keys, because those chords all have open strings. I will reemphasize this later.

C D E F G A B C -no #'s or ♭'s

G A B C D E F$^{\#}$G   1#

D E F$^{\#}$G A B C$^{\#}$D   2#'s

A B C$^{\#}$D E F$^{\#}$G$^{\#}$A   3#'s

E F$^{\#}$G$^{\#}$A B C$^{\#}$D$^{\#}$E   4#'s

B C$^{\#}$D$^{\#}$E F$^{\#}$G$^{\#}$A$^{\#}$B   5#'s

F$^{\#}$G$^{\#}$A$^{\#}$B C$^{\#}$D$^{\#}$E$^{\#}$F$^{\#}$ 6#'s

C#D#E#F#G#A#B#C#   7#'s

--- All of the key notes are up a 5th from the previous key.

We have completed the sharp keys. If you didn't notice, the order of sharps moves up in 5^{ths} as well as the keys.

Order of keys: (C), G, D, A, E, B, F♯, C♯
Order of sharps: F♯, C♯, G♯, D♯, A♯, E♯, B♯

Here's an easy way to remember the order of sharps using the guitar:
  F♯, C♯, G♯, D♯, A♯, E♯, B♯

Moving like the order of notes in a power chord.

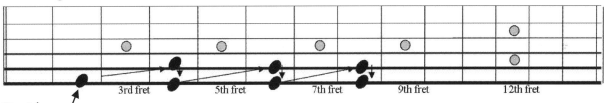

Start here

(You may take the sharps away to visualize the intervals and then add the sharps back in.)

Each sharp is a 5th away from each other. When you count this, each sharp you start on should be counted as number one.

F# is number one, G=2, A=3, B=4, and C#=5. Now start on C# and count up 5 tones to G#.

Continue this process with all of the sharps.

Remember : E# sounds as an "F" pitch but will be called E#.

            B# sounds as an "C" pitch but will be called B#.

Flat Keys

A flat lowers a pitch by half a step, or one fret. It is represented by the symbol : ♭ .

Once again we start at C major to visualize the naturally occurring half steps:

```
1       2       3       4       5       6       7       8
C       D       E       F       G       A       B       C
    1       1       1/2     1       1       1       1/2
```

Flat keys move in 4ths, so we do the same thing as before with the 5ths, but now moving in 4ths.

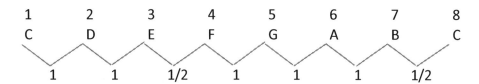

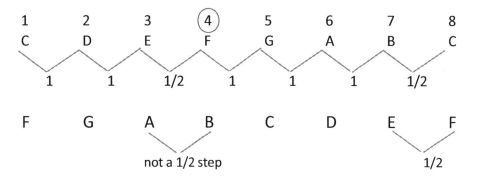

A to B is not a half step, so we flat (♭) or lower the B to B♭. This "fixes" the scale: F, G, A, B♭, C, D, E, F.

Note: <u>F is the only flat key that doesn't have "flat" in its name.</u>

Note: The flatted note B♭ is up a 4th and is the next key.

All of the Flat Keys: (We start with C to see 4ths)

C D E F G A B C   no #'s or ♭'s

F G A B♭ C D E F   1♭

B♭ C D E♭ F G A B♭   2♭'s

E♭ F G A♭ B♭ C D E♭   3♭'s

A♭ B♭ C D♭ E♭ F G A♭   4♭'s

D♭ E♭ F G♭ A♭ B♭ C D♭   5♭'s

G♭ A♭ B♭ C♭ D♭ E♭ F G♭   6♭'s

C♭ D♭ E♭ F♭ G♭ A♭ B♭ C♭   7♭'s

(Note: C♭ sounds as B, written as C♭. F♭ sounds as E, written as F♭).

Here again, there is a movement up in 4ths from key to key. Notice the sequence of flats move up in 4ths also. Order of Keys: (C), F, B♭,E♭,A♭,D♭,G♭,C♭

The Order of Flats: B$^\flat$, E$^\flat$, A$^\flat$, D$^\flat$, G$^\flat$, C$^\flat$, F$^\flat$

(You may take the flats away to visualize the interval and then add the flats back in.)

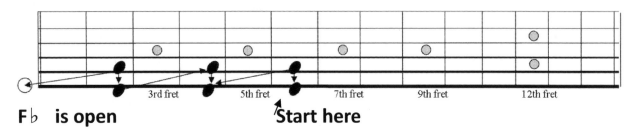

F$\flat$ is open   **Start here**

Review:

Sharp keys move up in 5^{ths} as well as the order of sharps.

Flat keys move up in 4^{ths} as well as the order of flats.

Let's look at a 5th:

C	D	E	F	G
1	2	3	4	5

❋ C to G is a 5th

Let's look at a 4th:

C	D	E	F
1	2	3	4

❋ C to F is a 4th

Remember that C $\rightarrow$ G is a 5th. Then what is G $\rightarrow$ C?

G$\rightarrow$C is a 4th. Although they are the same notes, they are in a different order, or inverted. Count the first note as one.

C$\rightarrow$G = 5th
G$\rightarrow$C = 4th

Thus:
The circle of 5^{ths} is an inversion or opposite of 4^{ths}. Very ingenious.

Space for notes

Intervals of Scale and Chord Tones

In addition to the knowledge of sharps and flats in the keys you are playing, we need to visualize the shapes of intervals on the guitar. Visualization with **Apophenia** is a key to recognizing what to play! Because of the way the guitar is tuned, shapes of intervals are repetitive all over the neck. We will start with chords. Look at the **SHAPES!**

A triad is a chord with three notes ("tri" = three, as in tripod or tricycle). More tones will be added later. We will only work with three now.

There are four chord types. **Major, minor, diminished,** and **augmented**. Notice the "shape" of the thirds. Here are examples of each type:

C major- *a major third with a minor 3rd on top*

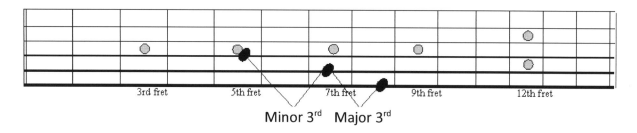

C minor- *a minor third with a major third on top*

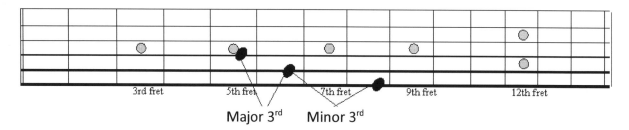

Diminished-*two minor thirds*

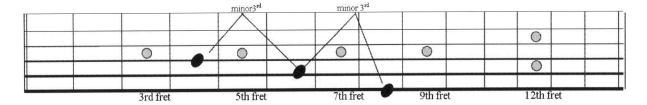

C Augmented-*two major thirds*

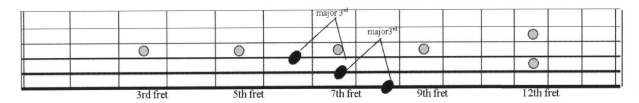

Below are the related notes to the diagrams in the previous section:

1. **Major chord:**   major 3rd with a minor 3rd on top
2. **Minor chord:**   minor 3rd with a major 3rd on top
3. **Diminished chord:**   minor 3rd with a minor 3rd on top
4. **Augmented chord:**   major 3rd with a major 3rd on top

Are you seeing the pattern? You may see there are major and minor thirds. Both exist in a major scale. A major third is two steps. A minor third is one and one-half steps. This is explained further in the next section.

Intervals of Scale and Chord Tones

The tuning of the guitar is in 4^{ths} (E, A, D, G, B, E), until we get to the third string. G to B is a major 3rd, so the shapes of the chords change. The major 3rd is on the same fret, instead of below it, like the other strings. We play a major 3rd by playing the 3rd string and the 2nd string on the same fret.

The tuning from the B string to the high E returns to the interval of a 4th. This tuning created the ability to have a two octave range across the neck of the guitar, without having to change positions.

Intervals of Scale and Chord Tones

If we begin to build the chords from the first string, you can visualize the shapes. Since we learned that chords are built in thirds, we can now see it on the guitar. The intervals involved are the root, the 3rd, and the 5th. Thirds may be either major or minor.

Major 3rd: 2 whole steps in the scale. Two steps= 4 frets.

Minor 3rd: 1 ½ steps in the scale or 3 frets above on the guitar. → (The minor 3rd is a lowered or flatted major 3rd).

Let's look at these chords:

There are three notes; the root, third (major or minor), and fifth. Fifths are called **perfect**, and are not called major or minor. (A lowered perfect fifth is **diminished**, while a raised perfect fifth is called **augmented**-more on this later). We are looking at **SHAPES** again!

A perfect 5th is 3$^{1/2}$ steps or 7 frets above.

C Major (CEG)

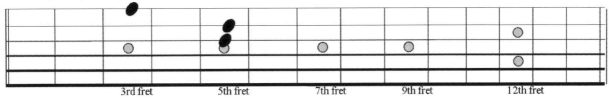

3rd fret   5th fret   7th fret   9th fret   12th fret

C minor (CE♭G)

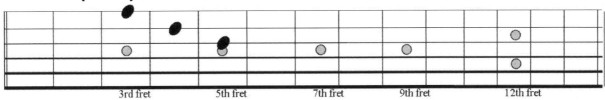

3rd fret   5th fret   7th fret   9th fret   12th fret

C+ (Augmented) (CEG#)

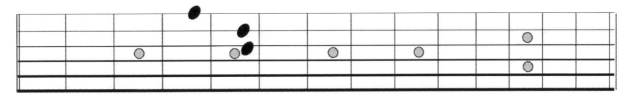

C° (Dim) (C E♭G♭)

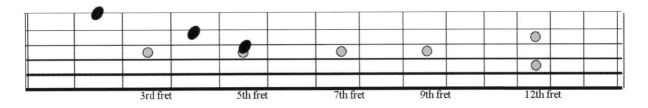

3rd fret   5th fret   7th fret   9th fret   12th fret

Notice that C° is written with flats. This is proper spelling. It is **E♭, not D#**. This is because we are writing in 3rds. C is one, D is two, and E is three, and flatted.

Although E♭ and D# are the same notes (enharmonic notes), the proper spelling is C, E♭, and G♭.

Chapter 2

Universal Chord Shapes – Major Shapes

We have reached the point of knowledge where we begin to build up and across the guitar. **You must know chapter 2 of the material before you move on.**

Do you recall that the three major chords in any major key are: I, IV, and V? These chords are going to be our main emphasis at this point. We will begin in G major. The **I, IV, and V will be G, C, and D**. We will be building three note chords; only working with three strings at a time, starting with the top three strings.

There are three major triad shapes. Each contains the three notes in the chord. Each shape is an inversion (or different stacking) of the notes from high to low.

Remember: We are not just learning chords, but chord tones as well. This is a necessary tool for improvisation. The best notes to play against a chord are the chord tones themselves! If you have been reading about music, these chord tones are called "arpeggios" if played one at a time. They are the notes of the chord only. You can think of this as three notes from a scale which contains eight notes.

Universal Chord Shapes – Major Shapes

We begin with I, IV, and V in G (G, C, and D). Starting with D, because it's position on the neck is the lowest available visual chord in the I, IV, and V series. This is familiar as the D chord, which was probably one of the first chords you learned on the guitar. We will also call this a **"D shape."** Visually, other chords will have the "D shape." Being that we are only playing three strings, we will be able to move this chord up the neck, as you will see shortly. Bottom to top: A,D,F#.

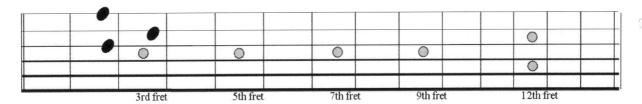

Below is a G chord. It is going to be associated with an **"F shape"** due to the fact that this is generally the first F chord you learned. We are moving this shape to the 3rd fret, which is a G chord. B,D,G.

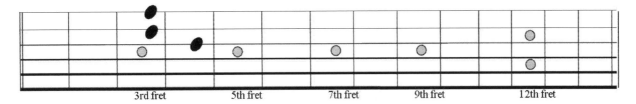

Below is a C chord. It will be associated with an **"A shape."** This is derived from the first A chord learned. The A chord has an open string, E, on top (the first string). In order to make this shape movable up the neck, the open string in the "A shape" becomes a fretted note as the chord is moved. C,E,G.

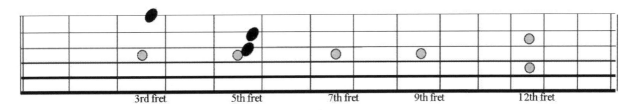

Universal Chord Shapes – Major Shapes

Beginning with the D chord (D shape) again, we will learn the inversions of the chords. Inversions are the same chords in a different order, or stacking of tones. The D chord (low to high) is: A, D, F$^\sharp$. The next inversion will be D, F$^\sharp$, A. Notice the chord tones are the same, only in a different order – inverted.

Note: If you are still learning the notes on the neck, you may not know this chord is being spelled: D, F$\sharp$, A; unless you go through the process of figuring out each note. It is not imperative that you know the notes, it will come in time. <u>The shape is what you want to concentrate on.</u>

The next D chord would repeat the 1st shape at the 14th fret, an octive higher than the D note we started with.

Going back to look at each D chord; notice the root of the chord (D) is on a different string in each inversion. This will help you to learn the position of the chords.

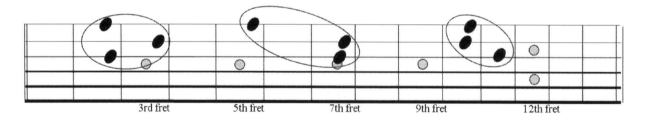

| 3rd fret | 5th fret | 7th fret | 9th fret | 12th fret |

Apophenia : <u>*The bottom note of EACH chord and the top note of the following chord is always shape #3!*</u> This will help you learn <u>*where*</u> the chords are located much faster. This will be an ongoing pattern as you go through this book.

Universal Chord Shapes – Major Shapes

We will now continue with the G and C chords. We move these up the neck through their inversions using the same chord shapes as the D chord.

The G chord starts with the "F shape," then uses the "D shape," and then the "A shape." ***Notice the "shape" order follows a pattern.*** *Even though you start with an F shape, the D shape always follows, and then the A shape.* It is like that with each chord (D, G, C) Inversions are (high to low): B D G; D G B; and G B D.

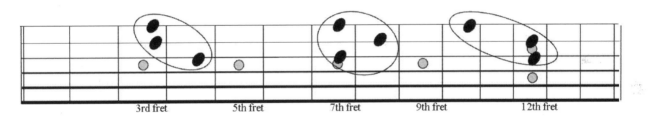

The C chord starts with the **"A shape"** and moves to **"F shape"** and then the **"D shape"**. These are the three inversions which are spelled: C E G, E G C, and G C E.

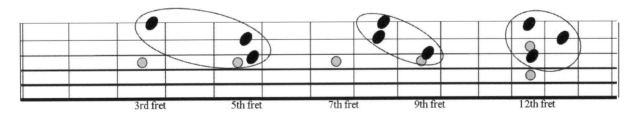

The order of shapes follows the same pattern! Shape #3 *always* applies between the bottom note (3rd string) of the first shape and the top note of the next chord to follow! This is *very* important!

All three chords and the inversions:

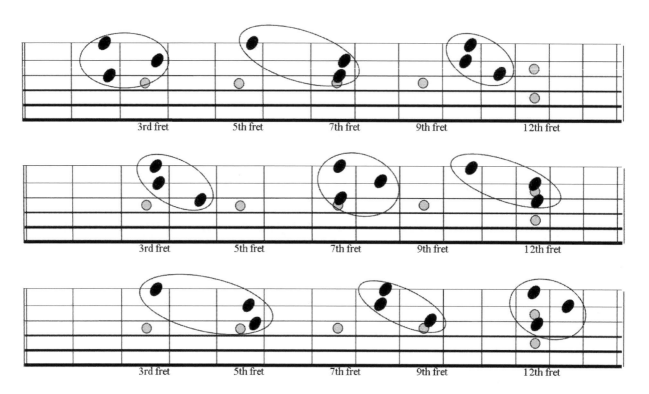

1) Play through inversions of each chord, until you know them and their location.

2) Starting with D, play in this order: D,G, and C through all inversions up the neck. You will be playing the first D,G, and C from the frames above. Then play the next D,G, and C. Then the last three, working your way up the neck. This sounds very musical.

Did you notice the common tones between the chords?

⊙D⃝F♯ A   V

Ⓖ B Ⓓ   I

C EⓊG⃝   IV

These are the only major chord shapes to be learned. Other chords, across the neck, will be learned through visual association shortly. Rather than learn I, IV, and V in every key, which will be an eventuality, let's take a more logical path.

Guitar players tend to play in certain keys. These chords being the ones that sound good on guitar. You may have noticed that many guitar songs are in the same keys.

Universal Chord Shapes – Major Shapes

The keys that guitar players use more often than others are: **C, G, D, A,** and **E. Notice how many open string chords are in these keys.**

Use these keys as a starting point in your study of the major chord shapes. Notice the repetition of chords in the following list of I, IV, and V for each key. **(Notice the circle of 5^{ths})**

C:	CFG	
G:	GCD	as listed above. You are doing this key first.
D:	DGA	
A:	ADE	
E:	EAB	

Because of the repetition of chords, you only need to learn the inversions of seven chords, rather than fifteen.

You can add other keys as you need them. It will be easier than the initial learning process.

Do not move on until you have at least these 5 keys down! **You will be using these chords throughout the book and need to know them.** ***These chords will also be applied to solo concepts. Chord on chord.***

Substitute these new chords in songs you know, playing the new chord shapes instead what you would normally play. This will increase your knowledge and most importantly, your speed.

space for notes

Universal Chord Shapes - Minor Chord Shapes

Now we will learn the minor chords using the same visual process. Three string chords with three recognizable shapes. In G minor, we will use i, iv, and v (all minor = lower-case) = Gm, Cm, and Dm.

We begin with Dm, which will be the **Dm shape**. It is the lowest chord available on the neck on the top three strings in this key. **The Dm shape is (low to high): A, D, and F.**

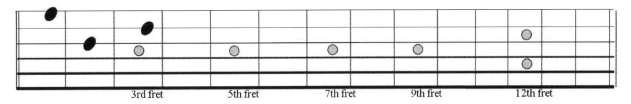

The next chord is Gm. This chord shape comes from the **Fm shape**, which would be located on the first fret. **The Gm is (low to high): B♭, D, and G.**

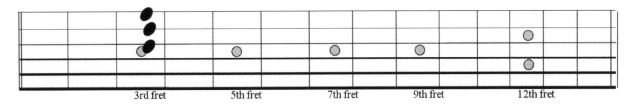

The Cm chord shape is derived from a **Bm shape**, one of the earliest chords learned. **The Cm chord is (low to high): C, E♭, and G.**

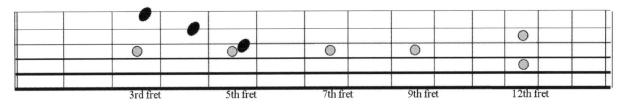

All chords will be moveable up the neck using three strings.

The following are Dm, Gm, and Cm. One chart for each chord.

Play each inversion of each chord up the neck. _Do you see shape #3 on the low note to high note from chord to chord?_

Play inversions of ascending chords in order up the neck. Dm, Gm, and Cm. Dm, Gm, and Cm. Gm, Dm, and Cm. This will take you to the Dm (Dm shape) an octave higher than your starting point – 13th fret.

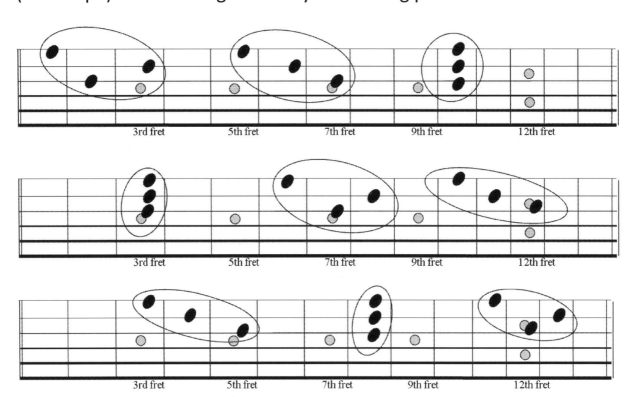

Guitar keys for minor chords as a starting point are:

Am (i, iv, v)	Am Dm Em
Em (i, iv, v)	Em Am Bm
Bm (i, iv, v)	Bm Em F#m
Gm (i, iv, v)	Gm Cm Dm as seen above. Learn this key first.
Cm (i, iv, v)	Cm Fm Gm

You may add the other keys when you are ready. **Do not move on until you know these five keys.** Practice in order the way you did major inversions. Thus Gm, Cm and Dm. Gm, Cm, and Dm. Gm, Cm, and Dm, so you see repeat shapes on Cm and Dm chords. Try using these in songs with the same chords.

Gradual Study -Relative minor

A discussion of "relative minor" is needed at this point.

Each major scale has a relative minor. Relative meaning related. The relationship is the same key signature and thus same notes.

C major has the relative minor of A minor. The relative minor may be found by counting up a 6th:

C	D	E	F	G	A	B	C
1	2	3	4	5	(6)	7	8

Or down a 3rd:

C	D	E	F	G	A	B	C
					(3)	2	1

C major and Am have the same key signature (no ♯'s or ♭'s). The scales contain the same notes. C major starts on C and Am starts on A. The difference is <u>where the half steps occur</u>, creating a minor tonality.

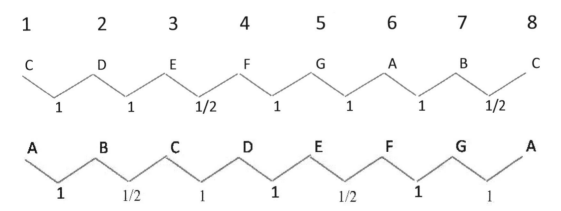

When playing the first three intervals of A minor, you should hear the minor quality of the scale.

Gradual Study

If you continue up the circle of 5^{ths}, G major has a relative minor of Em.

G	A	B	C	D	E	F#	G	
1	2	3	4	5	(6)	7	8	← G

E	F#	G	A	B	C	D	E	
								←Em

	Sharps Relative Minor		Flats Relative Minor
G	Em	F	Dm
D	Bm	B$^\flat$	Gm
A	F$^\sharp$m	E$^\flat$	Cm
E	C$^\sharp$m	A$^\flat$	Fm
B	G$^\sharp$m	D$^\flat$	B$^\flat$m
F$^\sharp$	D$^\sharp$m	G$^\flat$	E$^\flat$m
C$^\sharp$	A$^\sharp$m	C$^\flat$	A$^\flat$m

Notice the *enharmonic* scales above. Refer back to pages 13 and 16 if you are unsure of the enharmonic spelling.

Note: Minor scales played over the relative major chord will "sound" major because of the chord being played. This is another weapon to add to your arsenal!

CHAPTER 3

Inverting Major Chords

Rather than having to learn random chords all over the neck, you will learn by association. That is, you will always have a reference point with which to start. The **visualization** of the chord shape is imperative to memorization. **Shape #2 at the beginning of the book is the key here.** Do you remember finding the G notes using shape #2: (5th fret on the 4th string and 3rd fret on the 1st string?) This will be used exclusively in this study.

We will begin with the D chord (D shape) from the last section. The top note on the 1st string is F$^\sharp$. We will move that note down an octave using shape #2 (from learning all the notes exercise). The top note, F$^\sharp$, from the first chord is no longer used. Instead it's replaced by the lower F$^\sharp$. We will continue moving notes down now.

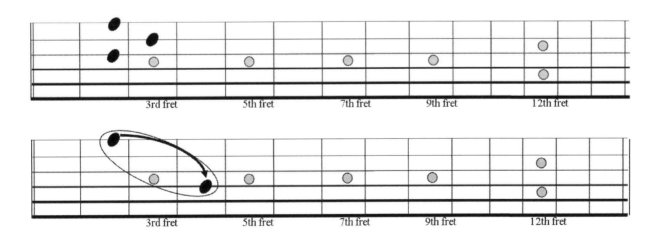

Can you visualize where the top note moves? Shape # 2.

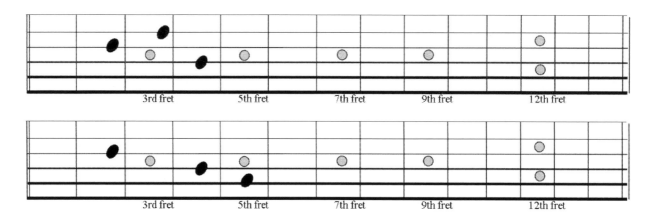

This is the additional shape of octave you learned before: **Shape #4.**

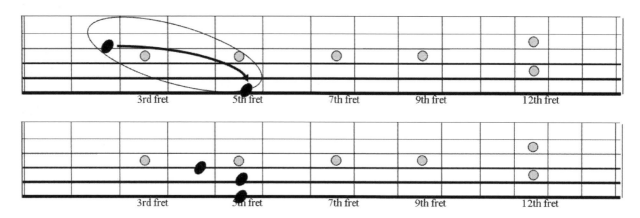

Note: Remember we are concentrating on triads (3 notes chords) for ease of learning.

It should be noted that the proper name of the first chord is D/F$^\sharp$. (D with an F$^\sharp$ in the bass, the first inversion. In conversation we would say "D over F sharp"). The second chord is D. The last chord is D/A. Names of chords will be covered later in the book.

Inverting Major Chords

The top note, F$^\sharp$, has been moved down an octave. The high note in the chord is now D. Move the D down an octave using shape #2. The high D is now not used. This is the next triad inversion.

The top note is now A (3rd string, 2nd fret). Moving this note down an octave will place the low A at 5th fret 6th string. This is the next inversion. These are all of the available inversions of this chord shape across the neck. Picture them three at a time.

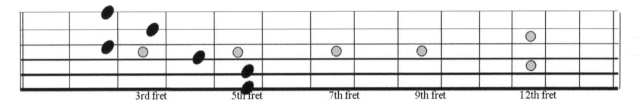

Note: By using a barre at the 2nd fret with your first finger, you can play all the tones except the low A. This is a very full sounding chord.

The next chord is the G (F shape). Move each tone down an octave, starting with the highest. You may notice that the inversions follow a G barre chord (3rd fret), except the low B, which is outside of the barre "box."

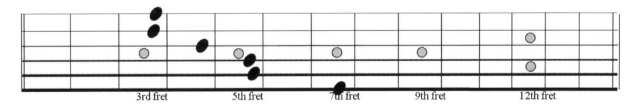

The next chord is the C (A shape). Move this chord down by also using the #2 shape. Take notice to the fact that this contains inversions inside of the barre chord C formed at the 3rd fret. This chord can be inverted down to the C (8th fret, 6th string). This may be played as a barre chord, omitting the high G on top (1st string).   (See next page)

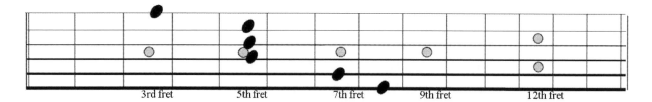

Inverting Minor Chords

Following the same procedure as the preceding section, we will create the minor chord inversions.

1.   Beginning with the Dm, lower the top note (F) down an octave using shape #2, the top F is no longer used as before.

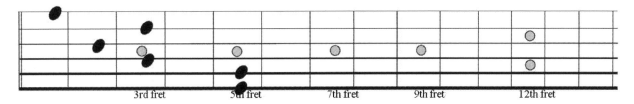

Note: Pay particular attention to the new triad shape (it looks like a D7). This can also be considered an incomplete F6 chord. F, A, and D. This is very useful in comping in blues, rock, and jazz.

Continue the inversion of Dm.

2. Invert the Gm (Fm shape) across the neck using shape #2.   Shape #4 for the last note.

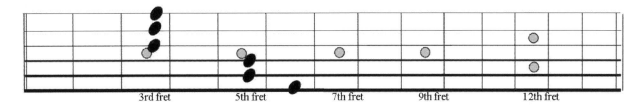

3.   Invert the Cm (Bm shape) across the neck using shape #2. Shape #4 for the last note.

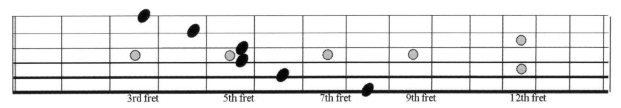

4.   Now you can use these inversions all over the neck. Do the guitar keys first and then move on to the other sharp and flat keys.

Inverting Minor chords

You have completed this phase. You have not just created chords but also a "map" of arpeggios. Arpeggios are chord tones rather than scale tones. Playing arpeggios over a chord is a very popular way to play, although it should be used at your discretion; a continuous stream of arpeggios ends up sounding isolated. Mixing arpeggios with scale tones sounds more polished.

Chapter 4

Seventh Chord Study

Any triad can be made into a seventh chord by adding another 3rd onto the triad. Thus we have root (1), third, fifth, and seventh.

A   C   E   G

R   3   5   7   ← This seventh is a minor 3rd above the 5th.

It is necessary to spell out seventh chords in a key to show the types available and their uses.

C E G B *major 3rd above the 5th*	C major 7 (Cmaj7,CΔ7)	IΔ7
D F A C minor 3rd above the 5th	D minor 7 (Dm7, D-7)	ii7
E G B D same as above	E minor 7 (Em7,E-7)	iii7
F A C E *major 3rd above the 5th*	F major 7 (Fmaj7, FΔ7)	IVΔ7
G B D F *MINOR 3rd above the 5th*	G7 "dominant" (G7)	V7
A C E G minor 3rd above the 5th	A minor 7 (Am7, A-7)	vi7
B D F A major 3rd above the 5th	Bm7(♭5) (B-7-5)	vii°7

NOTE: <u>B-7-5 is a half diminished chord (Ø)</u> .

Notice that the I and IV chords, C and F, are called the **major** 7th chords. The V7 chord is just called G7. It is the dominant meaning five. You should hear the difference.

Cmajor 7

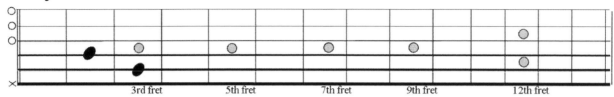

Fmajor 7

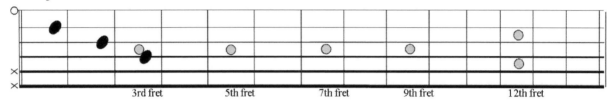

These are pretty chords and don't need to move or resolve anywhere. Now, let's play a basic G7 barre chord (The dominant, or V):

G7

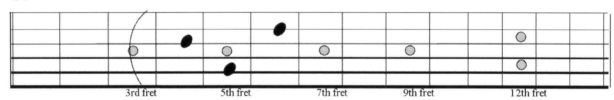

The G7 chord has tension in it. It needs to resolve, or finish, to another chord. That chord being C. Playing the G7 to C is very final sounding, like the end of a sentence; this is called a cadence. You may want to research more types of cadences in a theory book.

Let's look at the difference in these chords, and why they do what they do.

Cmaj7 = C E G B → Contains Em (EGB)

Fmaj7 = F A C E → Contains Am (ACE)

G7 = G B D F → Contains B° (BDF)

When you look inside the chord, there is a difference. There is a B° chord inside the G7. The B° chord is called the "leading tone" chord and needs to resolve to the I chord,"C ," because the leading tone tension.

Unresolved tension is like saying only half of a sentence. Note again that the major seventh chords just sit there and sound pretty. The G7 should resolve. **This is one of the most important areas in music.** The G7 is ONLY in the key of C. (Or C harmonic minor-more on this later).

Note: *What was "wrong" with Rock and Roll ? At its inception, Rock music was a new sound that many people didn't understand, and didn't like. It is common to play G7, C7, and D7 in a three chord song, or a 12 bar blues. G7 resolves to C. D7 resolves to G. The C7 never resolved to its I chord (F). This sound irritated the people who were always used to resolutions. They didn't know why, they just didn't like it. After 65 years of hearing this rock tonality, we have become accustomed to the sound and don't give it much thought.*

12 Bar Blues in G

Added note: You may want to avoid playing C7 in a 12 Bar Blues progression. That is your "tonal" decision. It is common to do so, but you may just play C without a seventh. This alleviates the "pull" of the C7 to want to resolve to F. I will commonly play both; perhaps two beats each, with the C being played last. It's your music so use your ear.

Being that the diminished and dominant 7th creates such tension, it is one of the most important chords and concepts to pursue.

Chapter 5

SEVENTH CHORD INVERSIONS- 1st three strings

This may not be quite as easy as the major and minor series. It will be, however, an essential addition to your playing. It will affect your accompanying and soloing extensively. Remember to <u>visualize these chord shapes</u>. We'll do three strings at a time again. You may be thinking "wait a second, there's four notes in a 7th chord!" You are right. But watch and listen. Play D7 this way: (note open string)

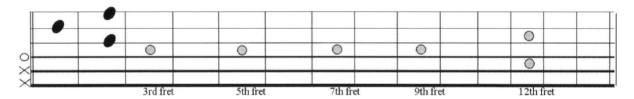

Now play D7 without the open D, 4th string. It still has tension. It's because of the diminished chord inside.

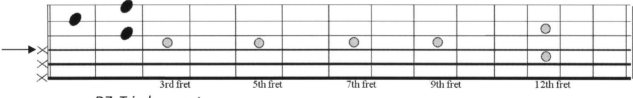

D7 Triad-no root

So - a great revelation – the incomplete chord has the same effect. I'm not saying "don't play the D." It will be easier to visualize these as triads. We are now playing (play 4th string and D7 again) D A C F♯. In diatonic (scale) order; it is D F♯ A C. You may play any three tones in the chord as long as you play the 7th (C). The C has to be in there. You can leave out any other note. (You may hear that the 3rd and the 7th notes are the strongest tones. These are called "guide tones." I consider these as the best sounding inversions).

We will learn these in order. Play D7 without the D again. We have A C F♯. Look at the order of notes in D7 → D F♯ A C. We have an A on the bottom. The next inversion up the neck will have C on the bottom, then eventually D, and then F♯. *Notice shape #3 from chord to chord.*

Note: This will also help you learn the fretboard notes more quickly .

Notes from bottom to top:

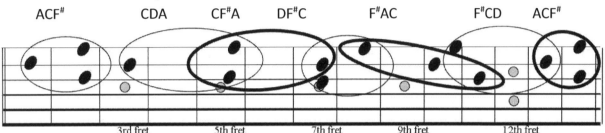

(The heavier marked lines help to show overlapped tones).

Visually note what each inversion looks like and where the next inversion is in relation to another. ***You may call the shapes whatever you wish.*** Using *apophenia*, I named each of these as how I saw them:

D7 shape

"Big" D7

Inverted big D7

Straight across +1

Diminished C (I am thinking of the seventh of the chord I had just used)

6th +7 (I am thinking : F♯ to D is a 6th shape, and C is the 7thof D)

D7 shape

   Use these chords in your playing as quick fills or in songs to allow you to remember them easier. A restatement or playing a quick chord during a solo is an effective tool.

Approaching a seventh chord from a 1/2 step below and sliding the chord into position is a good bluesy tool. (ex: F#7 sliding to G7).

 Space for Notes

Chapter 6

Seventh Chord Inversions- 2nd, 3rd, and 4th strings

We will go through more inversions of seventh chords. **The inversions on 2nd, 3rd, and 4th strings will also be incomplete.** You may add other chord tones later. This series of chords is the most useful due to the tonal range of the chord. They are in the center of the guitar's range, thus they are not too muddy or too high . These are referred to as inside rhythm chords, and they are great for accompaniment with other instruments or solo guitar. Visualize these shapes. They also make great licks if you play them one note at a time.

We will start with G7 on the 3rd fret. You may see this as part of the G7 you normally play as a barre chord .

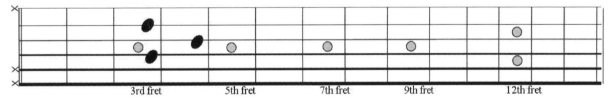

3rd fret   5th fret   7th fret   9th fret   12th fret

There is no root in this inversion.

As before, there are four inversions of this chord. But keep looking, because you may find more. Some inversions will not sound as good as others, depending on the order of tones. You may choose to avoid these inversions or only use them as passing changes. An example of passing changes would be to play four inversions of a chord in a measure, as opposed to just playing one.

Remember playing those inversions one note at a time is a nice little lick that is a restatement of the chord.

The inversion we are starting with has the F on the bottom. G7 is spelled G B D F. We will build the next inversion on G, then B, D, and we are back to F, an octave higher. You will notice there are two inversions with G in the bass here. One doesn't sound as good as the other and may be avoided. Use your ear. Another consideration is fingering when moving from one chord to another. Is one perhaps "not flowing" when moving from chord to chord? When using these in a solo context, all inversions should be considered.

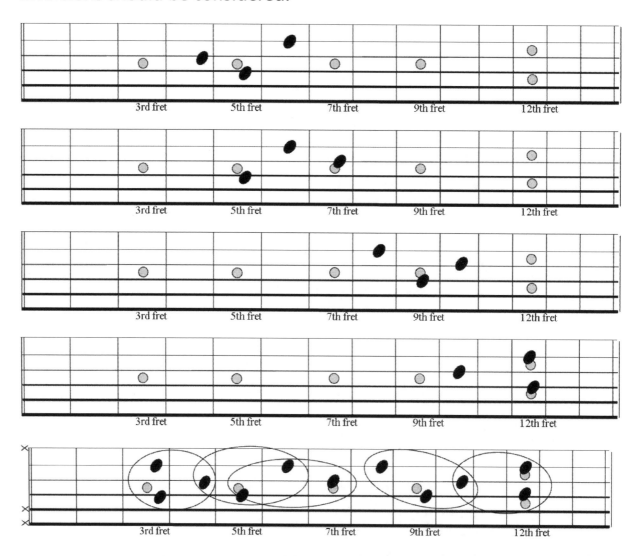

I "see" these shapes: D shape. 3+7. Power chord & one in the middle.
Dm shape. Big D7. I am using apophenia to remember them.

Now we will do G7, C7, and D7 starting in third position. Each of the following chords are inversions from above. We are looking at these chords as we will use them. Everything is in position.

Complete: G7 = G B D F   C7 = C E G B$^{\flat}$ D7 = D F$^{\sharp}$ A C

The inversions below are incomplete.

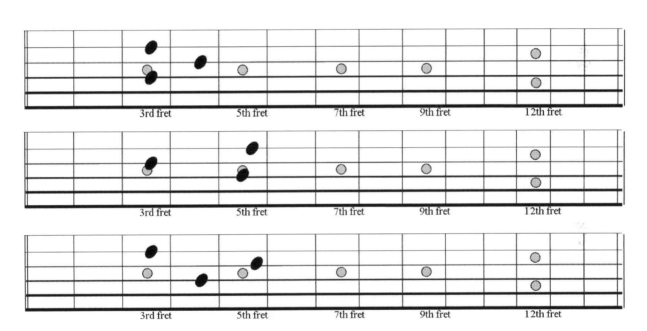

Play G7, C7, and D7 in 3rd position. Notice the closeness of the chords to each other. There is not a lot of hand movement from chord to chord.

Play G7, C7, and D7 in each position; G7, C7, and D7 in 3rd position, 5th position, etc. until you know them all in every key. Start with the guitar keys first.

Rather than having these written out in the text, I want you to learn them on your own. Remember that the shapes always follow the same patterns! They are just in different places. I hope that you may see other inversions also. Take the time to look for more. You should now be able to name most notes on the fret board quickly. Recognize your weaknesses and practice to make them a strength!

Space for notes

Chapter 7

Seventh Chord Inversions- 3rd, 4th, and 5th strings

You may, or may not find these as useable as the other inversions. There is more heaviness in these chords and tonally they don't stand out as much. However, they are not to be avoided, because they are part of a bigger picture. You may find them more useful as solo parts than chords. They are great for comping with a horn section.

We will start with C7 this time. The chord that we start within each section is determined by where they are positioned on the neck.

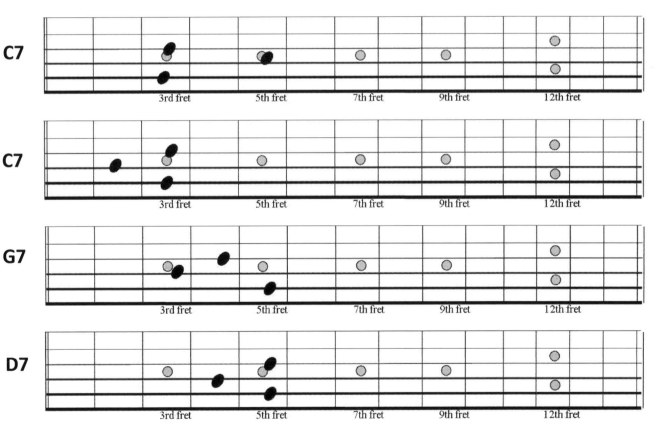

Here are a few inversions. Look for more on your own.

Play these as before: G7, C7, and D7 in each position. Learn in the guitar keys, and then move to others.

Chapter 8

Moving Seventh Chord Inversions Across the Neck – High To Low

By now, you should know at least all the seventh chord shapes on the 1st, 2nd, and 3rd strings in the guitar keys. You should also know 2nd, 3rd, and 4th string inversions and 3rd, 4th, and 5th string inversions.

Now let's move the inversions across the neck from high to low. There are two ways to do this. You may visualize each inversion as you have learned them; or you may see them as interconnected from inversion to inversion using shape #2 and #4. Both ways work. Let's use D7.

Example:

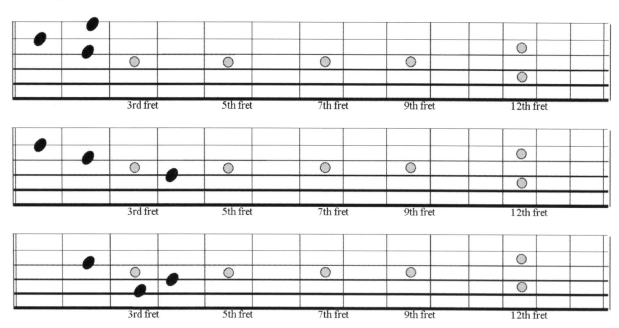

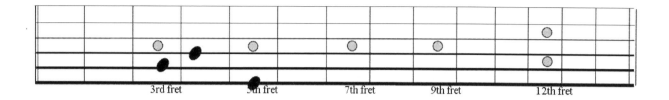

3rd fret   5th fret   7th fret   9th fret   12th fret

3rd fret   5th fret   7th fret   9th fret   12th fret

Chapter 9

Introduction to Other Chords – 9th, 11th, and 13th

(root, 3rd, 5th, 7th, 9th, 11th, 13th)

As an introduction to the "big" chords, we must look at chords from a guitarist's viewpoint. We are limited in the number of notes we can play simultaneously. As you can see, a 13th chord contains seven notes. Seven notes on a six string instrument poses a slight problem! A guideline for omitting notes in larger chords may be studied from a theory source.

We will approach these chords differently, because not all inversion building is possible (like the prior inversions). A chord with the 7th, 9th or 13th in the bass in the bass may not tonally effective, and in some cases, even physically playable.

Chapter 10

Seventh Chord Inversions You Have Learned
Adding 9th, 11th, and 13th tones

You should be able to play the seventh chord inversions from memory by now. At this point we will concentrate on the upper register chords and add upper extensions to the chords. The lower chord inversions will not stand out as well in some playing situations. They should be remembered though, for both solo lines and arpeggios.

We will begin with, the 2nd, 3rd, and 4th string seventh inversions. These are obviously not the only way to play those chords, but we are building on what you already know. Remember these shapes, played one note at a time, make great little licks with a lot of harmonic content. Let's start with G7. It is not my intention to show you everything available. Learning these on your own will provide better retention.

 As you will see, the notes we are adding will be A (9th), C (11th), and E (13th). Use G7 voicings* (inversions) that enable you to reach the additional note, or extentions. These higher voicings sound great when accompanying. Remember – if you are playing several bars of G, embellish each bar with 9ths, 11ths, and 13ths. It will add a lot of color to your playing. Use discretion. You may want to avoid certain voicings that may interfere with a sung or played melody. Playing a G9 (with an A on top) with the melody on G or B may create conflict. Use your ear. The melody is the controlling factor in note choice.

*Voicings- the vertical spacing of notes or pitches.

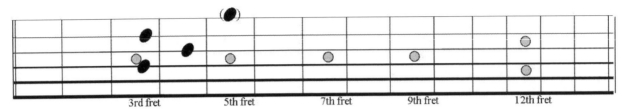

G9   The added note is the 9th, **A.** There is no root.

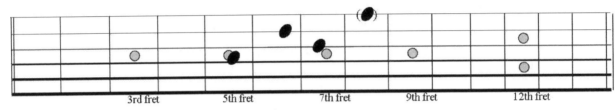

G11   The added note is the 11th, **C.**

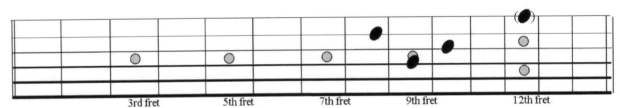

G13 The added note is the 13th, **E.**   Nice wide voicing!

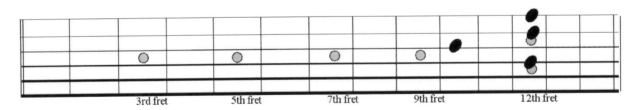

G13 (No root)   Another nice voicing!

You should now work with lower inversions and begin adding the 9ths, 11ths, and 13ths. As you become more comfortable, increase the number of tones in the chords.

Chapter 11

Large Chord Structure – the internal workings of a chord

As you have seen, we have been playing parts of a chords rather than the entire chord. Incomplete chords still function as if it were a complete chord. Obviously, the more harmonic content present, the richer the sound. In many cases presented here, we are "voicing" with the consideration that another instrument would be playing the root note. As in the following case:

You should understand that adding 3rds above a triad creates 7th, 9th, 11th, and 13th chords. Let's look at the total package.

A complete G13 chord: GBDFACE

What is INSIDE the G13?

Let's spell it out in triads. The chord tones are listed in triads.

G B D = G major
B D F = B°
D F A = Dm
F A C = F major
A C E = Am
C E G (adding the root again on top) = C major

E G B (adding the root and the 3rd again)= Em

This is every chord in the key of C!

G13 as seventh chords (4 notes):

G B D F – G7

B D F A – Bm7♭5

D F A C – Dm7

F A C E – F major 7

A C E G – Am7

C E (G B) – C maj7   by adding root and third again on top.

E G B D - Em7

G13 as ninth chords (5 notes)

G B D F A – G9

B D F A C –the C (♭9) extension is not normally added.

D F A C E – Dm9

F A C E G - F major9

A C E G B – Am9

C E G B D – C major9

E G B D F – Em9

Need we take it further? Hopefully you can see that playing these chord extensions above the root create these large chords. If your bassist or other guitar player is playing a G root, or G chord, G7 etc, you can play an Fmaj7 arpeggio or Fmaj7 chord over what they are playing to create this huge chord tonality. It is another way of thinking and breaking out of the same old scale usage. You may hear jazz players playing all the chord extensions in solos (and the altered extensions-more later), and never playing the root. This is an invaluable tool. This all goes back to chords. You have to practice scales for dexterity, but you don't play

note for note scales when you solo (hopefully). The best notes you can play against a chord are the chord tones. This doesn't mean you should play constant arpeggios either. Have a friend play a G chord. You play each note of a G major scale, holding each note for several seconds. Listen to each note and the effect of each note. You will notice two notes don't work well. Why? They are in the scale. It is the note's effect on the chord that creates this "atonality." The C and the F♯ in the scale you probably noticed, didn't work well. They work in passing, but not if you linger on them.

Think of the G chord again G B D – when you play a C note, the chord's B tone sounding with the C – you have notes a ½ step apart. An octave higher C, the effect is somewhat decreased but still there. The F♯ is the leading tone, or major seventh. The root is only a half step away. It is good for a passing note but not to linger on, <u>UNLESS</u> it is contained in the chord. The G major 7 chord would contain the F♯.

Thus: More power to the chord tones.

Chapter 12

The Dominant Chord Secret of the Universe

We have seen that the dominant (V) chord's mission is to resolve to the root (I) chord. The V7 form makes it ever stronger because of the diminished chord inside it.

"The V chord can be altered in any way" *(and still function as a dominant chord).* That means no matter what you do to it, it will still resolve! ♭5, ♯5, ♭9, ♯9, ♯11, ♯5♯9, or 13♭9. They all resolve.

To make a long story short, if you take a series of V to I chords in succession, there is a continuous tension, resolution, tension, resolution. Suppose our key is C. The V7 is G7. What is a fifth above G? D. What is a fifth above D? A. What is a fifth above A? E. We can alter the V7 any way, right? So we start at E7, from C, and work toward C.

C → E7 → A7 → D7 → G7 → C
(Any altered version)

What we are doing is a succession of key changes to get to C by using a cycle of five.
We are "borrowing" Chords from another key.

E7 is the V7 of A
A7 is that V7 of D
D7 is the V7 of G
G7 is the V7 of C

So I can make the E7 an E13♭9 and it still works. Then we can vary each of the other chords, except the C (where the progression resolves or ends).

"So are you telling me I can solo that way?" How do you play a

G13 (♭9♭5) scale? (G13-9-5) We are in C (no sharps). Here is one approach:

We start on G: (We will call G the root because it is the chord root).

C scale from G:	Altered scale G-13 (♭5♭9):
G – Root	G – Root
A – 2/9	**A**♭ **– ♭9**
B – 3	B – 3
C – 4/11	C -4/11
D – 5	**D**♭ **– ♭5**
E – 6/13	E-13
F – minor7	F – minor7
G – Octave Root	G – Octave Root

Alter the notes as needed to complete the scale of your choice to match it's chord.

This may be a lot to digest. If you start with the smaller chords, you can create the altered scales. You must know your fret board and the notes in the chord.

Chapter 13

Open Chord Voicings

The previous triads we studied were closed voicings. The tones followed each other in scale succession with small intervals between the notes. A closed voicing is written in notation with the notes within an octave range. Here are two that we have learned written in notation.

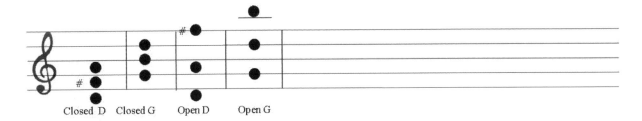

Closed D   Closed G   Open D   Open G

(For visual purposes, the stems have been omitted from the above).

In these open voicings, the middle tone jumps up an octave and there are "open spaces" between the tones. All chords forms; major, minor, diminished, and augmented can be opened. The sound is very full with an open chord. There will be skipped strings presented in these voicings. These should be muted. It is easier to just play the notes with your fingers. This provides simultaneous tones rather than a strum.

The first chord is G in all inversions. Remember all the chord shapes will look the same in other keys, only on different frets. The three tones are never on adjacent strings.

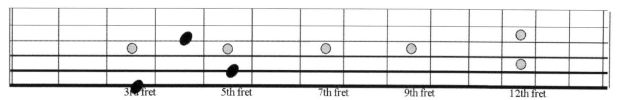

G opening voicing (root position) 3ʳᵈ is up a 10ᵗʰ

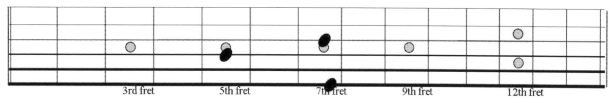

G opening voicing (1ˢᵗ inversion)

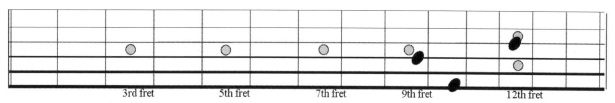

G opening voicing (2ⁿᵈ inversion)

Now A minor

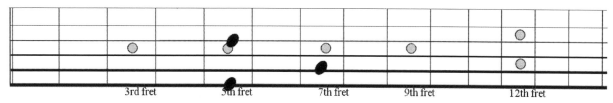

Am open voicing (root position)

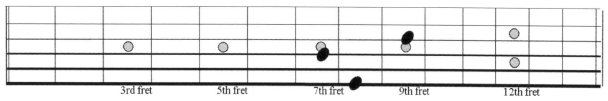

Am open voicing (1ˢᵗ inversion)

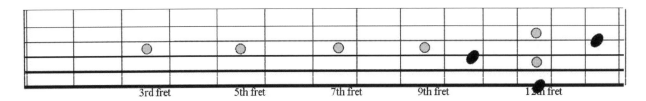

Am open voicing (2ⁿᵈ inversion)

These are the available forms of major and minor triads on 6ᵗʰ, 5ᵗʰ, and 4ᵗʰ strings. Move these across the neck to other strings. Do major and minor, augmented, and sevenths in all keys.

The diminished chord remains the same in appearance on the low strings. Remember these chords repeat themselves in minor 3rds (1 ½ steps) and any note may be considered the root!

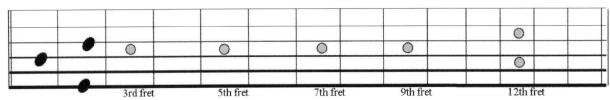

Diminished   - may be called F#, G♭, A , D#, or E♭.

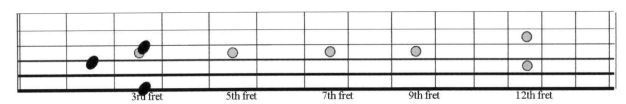

Diminished   - may be called G, B♭, A#, E, or F♭.

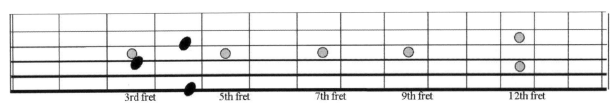

Diminished   - may be called A♭, G#, B, C♭, F, or E#.

Moving to the 5th fret repeats the chord played on the second fret. It is then repeated at the 8th fret, and then 11th fret. These are the diminished inversions. They are a minor third apart.

Visualization to This Point

You should have grasped the concept of this book. It is now that you should review and add other chord tones to the triads you have learned. You will be visualizing a combination of two chord forms that you have learned. Combine the inversion shapes across the neck so that are using a combination of two inversions. When you add one note to a triad, you will have two triads. Play a C chord. (CEG adding B gives you Cmaj7. The E,G, and B is an Em chord; two triads). Find them everywhere you can.

 Keep extending the chord tones as far as you can in each position that you play them. This should speed up the knowledge of the fret board dramatically.

Chapter 14

The Complete G13 Arpeggio

Here is the complete G13 arpeggio as it occurs on the neck.

(Key of C: V13)

G - root

B – major 3rd

D – 5th

F – minor 7th

A - 9th

C - 11th

E – 13th

The first arpeggio begins on the 6th string and starts and ends on the root G. Notice the C chord sitting on top of the arpeggio.

G13 arpeggio G to G Sixth string start. (GBDFACE)

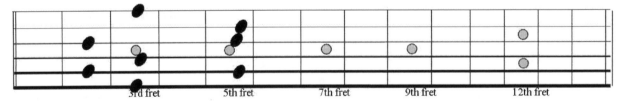

G13 arpeggio –note the C chord on top:

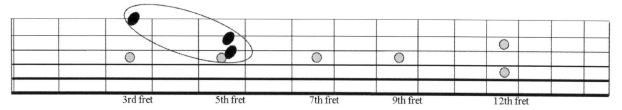

G13 arpeggio on the 5th string start.

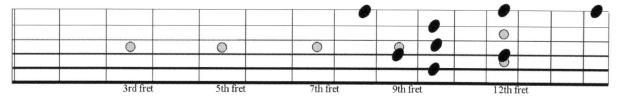

G13 arpeggio – notice F chord sitting on top:

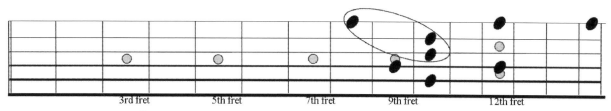

G13 arpeggio 4th string startG13 arpeggio – note Dm chord on top:

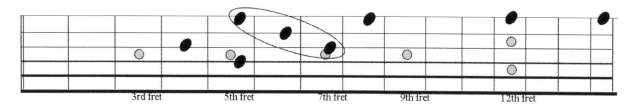

ANY part of this arpeggio may be played over a G or G7, G9, etc. It will add a unique essence to your playing. This is an important concept of this book! Chord on chord soloing gives you larger intervals, rather than half and whole steps in a standard scale. Learn to play the arpeggios out of order so they don't sound like arpeggios. This is easily done by string skipping. In the last two arpeggios pictured, notice the pattern on the strings. Strings 3, 1, and then 4, 2, and lastly 3, 1. You would want to resolve the last note C to one of the G chord target tones. Playing the whole sequence backwards starting on the C enables you land on B, the third in the G chord. Make your own sequence. Can you see a D7 shape , then D shape ? There is string skipping, but the shapes are there. They are part of the Dm shape sitting on top of the arpeggio. *Then, take any three notes in the arpeggios on adjacent strings and determine the chord name.*

The notes played in these sequences create an element of surprise for the listener, and creates interest.

When phrasing, be aware of your timing and that you end in time. Make use of space between phrases. Don't create run-on sentences.

Learning to play good phrases is an art in itself. Limiting the number of notes in your phrases tends to let you to play something more musical. Remember the usage of target tones, hammer ons, pull offs, slides, vibrato, accents, changes in volume with picking, the length of notes, bends, and most importantly SPACE. Let the listener breathe. The multitude of different ways you can play four or five notes is quite amazing.

Chapter 15

Harmonic Minor Study

For this study we will use E harmonic minor. E harmonic minor is the E minor scale with a raised (sharped) 7th.

Em (natural) – [relative minor of G minor]:   E F$^\sharp$ G A B C D E

Em harmonic: E F$^\sharp$ G A B C D$^\sharp$ E

If you are unfamiliar with this scale, you may consult other sources in the fingerings of these scales. We are concerned here only with harmonic content, and of course, apophenia.

As we have done before with the major scale, we will now harmonize the scale in 3rds to create chords.

First let's look at Em natural: E F$^\sharp$ G A B C D

E G B = i	Em
F$^\sharp$ A C = ii°	F$^{\sharp\circ}$
G B D = III	G
A C E = iv	Am
B D F$^\sharp$ = v	Bm
C E G = VI	C
D F$^\sharp$ A = VII	D

These chords are exactly the same as G major. Em is now our i chord. Notice i, iv, and v are all minor chords.

69

E Harmonic Minor: E F$^\sharp$ G A B C D$^\sharp$

E G B – i	Em
F$^\sharp$ A C – ii°	F$^{\sharp}$°
G B D$^\sharp$ - III+	<u>G+ (augmented, $^\sharp$5)</u>
A C E – iv	Am
B D$^\sharp$ F$^\sharp$ - V	<u>B major</u>
C E G – VI	C major
D$^\sharp$ F$^\sharp$ A - vii°	<u>D$^{\sharp}$°</u>

Let's discuss the chords here. In the Em and F$^{\sharp}$° there is no change from E natural minor. (The i and ii° chords).

Next we have a G augmented chord. Remember this is two major 3rds, one on top of the other. The III+ chord, written: G+

The iv chord Am – no change

The V chord, B, has been altered to become a major chord. This is very important. If you play Em, Bm, and Em again you will see that the resolving "power" of the Bm as the v chord is minimal. Now play Em, B major, and then Em again. There is quite a difference in tension (from the B) to the release, or resolution to the Em. This is part of the brilliance of harmonic minor. The D$^\sharp$ inside of the B major chord wants to resolve, (or finish), up to E

The VI chord C – no change.

The vii° chord is D#°. **Now we have our second appearance of a diminished chord in the same key.** Both F#° and D#°. The D#° being the leading tone chord, "leads" to the root chord, Em.

Let's look at F#°, B major, and D#° chords.

F# A C

B D# F#

D# F# A

Notice the common tones here. If we were to make B into a B7, we would have: B D# F# A. This is a very strong chord resolving to Em.

Making the B7 into a B7-9, we would have: B D# F# A C.

This B7-9 now has both diminished chords inside of it.

(B) D# F# A and F# A C

Remember that any note in a diminished chord may be considered the root. Also diminished chords repeat themselves every minor 3rd up the neck, or 1 and a 1/2 steps .

This means that the F#° and the D#° are essentially the same chord.

Chapter 16

A Very Visual Approach to E Harmonic Minor

I chose to use E harmonic minor for the lack of many sharps. I will approach this as if I were playing an Em harmonic scale from E. (Fifth string, seventh fret)

I will lay out the scale first so you see the region of our work on the neck.

Em Harmonic scale

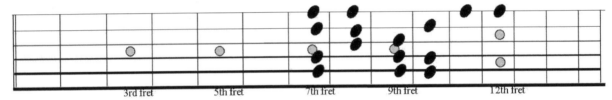

Now the visual part; here again are the chords:

Em

F#°

G+

Am

B

C

D#°

I am choosing the Em, B, C, and G+ chords to begin. You will immediately see why.

Em

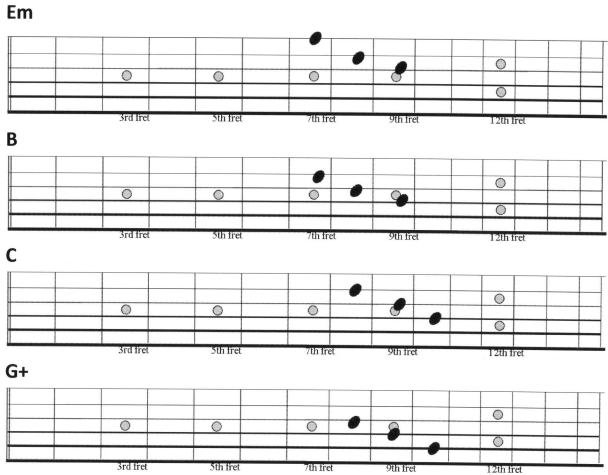

B

C

G+

They all look alike! APOPHENIA! If you now play each chord, one note at a time, moving from chord to chord, you will see you already have captured the tonal essence of the scale. Now you must lay out the rest of the entire group of chords in several inversions.

B

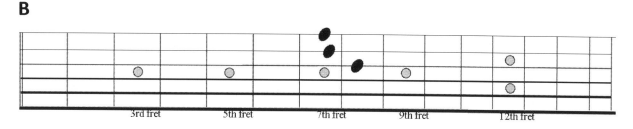

You may also choose to visualize and use B7 forms. How many can you find in this area of the neck? ***Note: Combining G+ and B triads = G+7.***

You may also use 4 or 5 note chords. An example: starting with Em, (Play as a seventh position barre chord, bottom to top).

E   5 st. 7fr
B   4 st. 9fr
E   3 st. 9fr
G   2 st. 8fr
B   1 st. 7fr

Remember! There are three inversions here.

This is only a starting point for you. You need to find every Em on the neck and build all of the above chords as closely as possible to that chord. You will begin to "matrix" these associations with apophenia and see shapes up and down the neck. This is a lot of work but the results will be worth every bit of study.

What I mean is this: When you choose any Em chord to start this exercise, where is the absolute closest Am, G+, etc.

We will do more of this in the next section.

Chapter 17

Exercise your new Knowledge

Let's work with a song that has more than three chords.

Do your exercise this way: Your chords are C, Am, Dm, and G7.

Play these chords starting on the C at 3rd fret – 3 strings only.

C

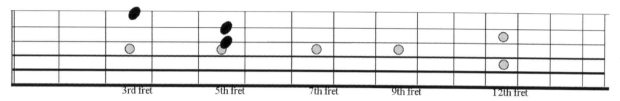

Am

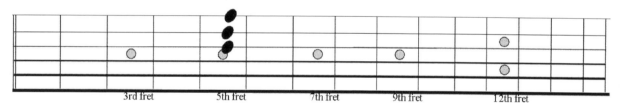

Dm

G7

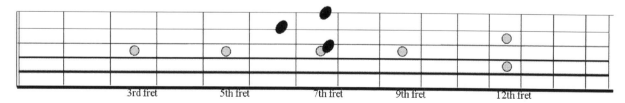

C

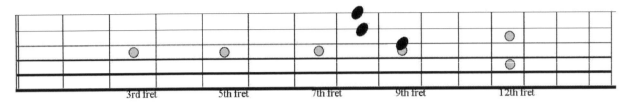

Am

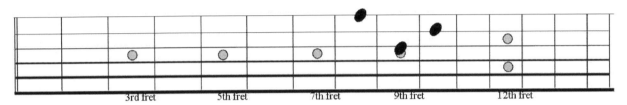

Dm

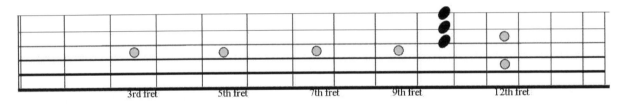

G7

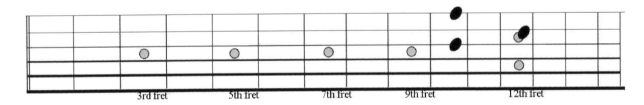

Let's move to another key: G Em Am and D7 using 2nd, 3rd, and 4th strings. **Finish the rest of the inversions. They are purposely left blank.** <u>**Keep the chords as close to each other as possible!**</u>

G

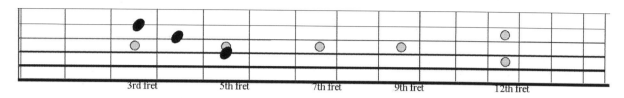

Em

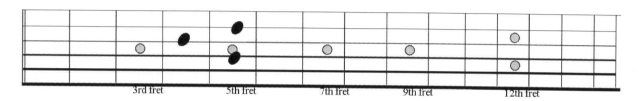

Am

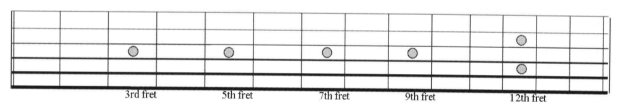

D7

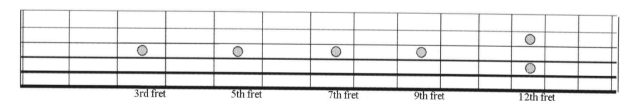

G

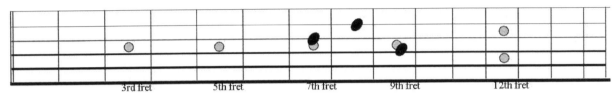

3rd fret 5th fret 7th fret 9th fret 12th fret

Em

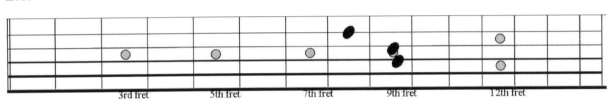

3rd fret 5th fret 7th fret 9th fret 12th fret

Am

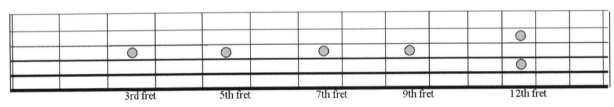

3rd fret 5th fret 7th fret 9th fret 12th fret

D7

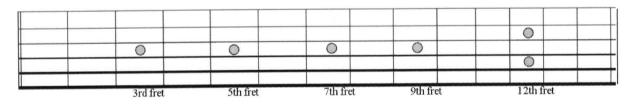

3rd fret 5th fret 7th fret 9th fret 12th fret

Next move up to the next G inversion on the same strings. Play the G, Em, Am, and D7. Then move the inversions across the neck to the 3rd, 4th, and 5th strings. If you aren't able to do this, review your inversions. If you are not sure that a particular inversion is correct, play the chord where you know it is correct and compare it the sound of the questionable chord. **You need to be able to complete this chapter.**

Another key, let's try E$^\flat$ on the 3rd, 4th, and 5th strings

E$^\flat$

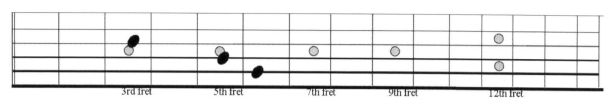

Cm

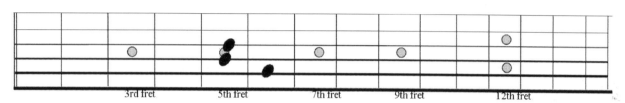

Fm

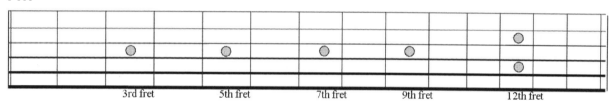

B$^\flat$ **7**

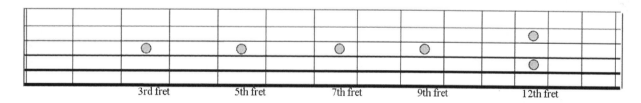

E♭

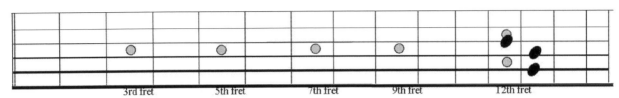

3rd fret   5th fret   7th fret   9th fret   12th fret

Cm

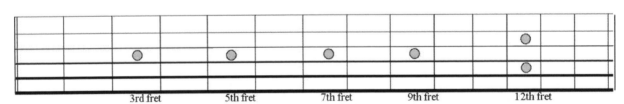

3rd fret   5th fret   7th fret   9th fret   12th fret

Fm

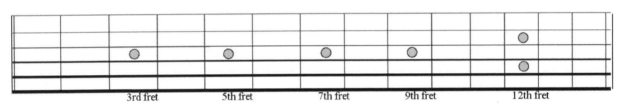

3rd fret   5th fret   7th fret   9th fret   12th fret

B♭ **7**

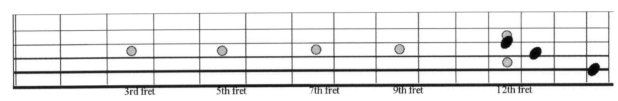

3rd fret   5th fret   7th fret   9th fret   12th fret

Make up your own exercises. Make them more difficult, it will be more beneficial and you will find much more information than we have touched on here.

You should begin working on teaching yourself altered (Flat 5, raised 5, 9, 11, 13, etc.) chords across the neck also. A four string approach may be needed depending on the chord.

Exercise in Naming Chords

As we have mentioned before, it is important that you are able to name chords from the notes they contain. Write down the notes and look for 3^{rds}. You should find at least one 3rd between the notes. That will be the starting point for constructing the root of the chord and naming it.

Name the chord :

A, G$^\sharp$, C$^\sharp$, from bottom to top (4th, 3rd, and 2nd string. Frets 2, 1, and 2). Look for 3^{rds}.

A → G$^\sharp$ not a 3rd
A → C$^\sharp$ is a 3rd

If we think of "A" as the root what is the relationship of G$^\sharp$ to A? Write out an A major scale if necessary. The G$^\sharp$ is the major 7th in the scale.

A = root
C$^\sharp$ = major 3rd
G$^\sharp$ = major 7th

A C$^\sharp$ (E) G$^\sharp$

The E is the missing tone. If we add the open 1st string, we have a complete Amaj7. You will play many incomplete chords on guitar.

Chapter 18

Exercise in Moving Chords Part 2

Let's move the D shape across the neck. Will it work? I will name the chords for you.

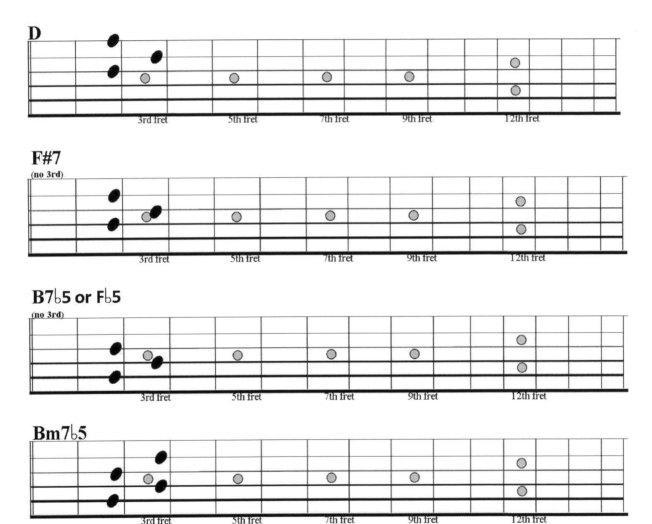

F#7♭5

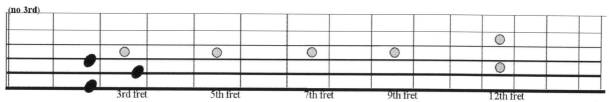

Now the Dm shape

Dm

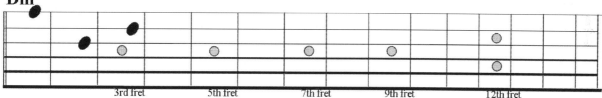

C7

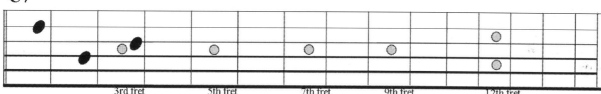

Moving this shape across results in unusual sounding chords. Can you name them?

The F shape on G

G

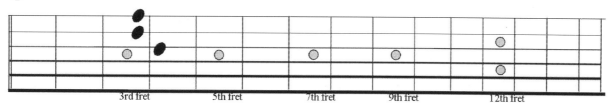

F#aug

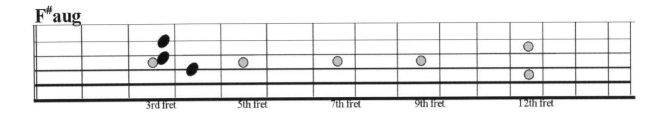

3rd fret   5th fret   7th fret   9th fret   12th fret

C#6

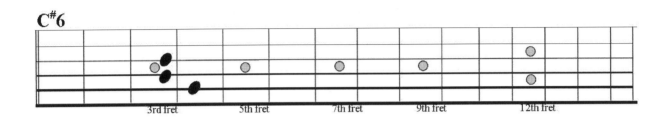

3rd fret   5th fret   7th fret   9th fret   12th fret

G#6

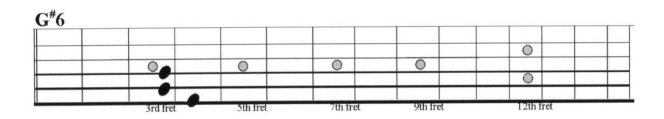

3rd fret   5th fret   7th fret   9th fret   12th fret

The A shape on C

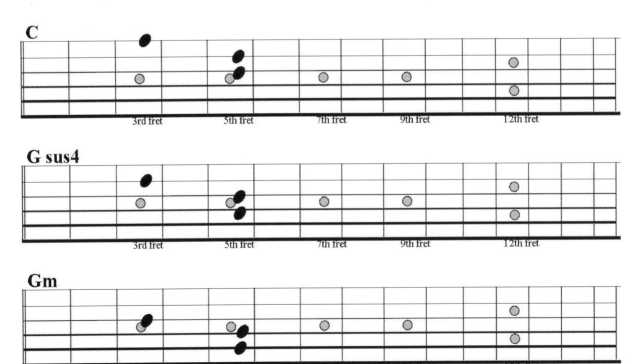

C

3rd fret   5th fret   7th fret   9th fret   12th fret

G sus4

3rd fret   5th fret   7th fret   9th fret   12th fret

Gm

3rd fret   5th fret   7th fret   9th fret   12th fret

Dm

3rd fret   5th fret   7th fret   9th fret   12th fret

Now do:

The Bm shape on Cm: Strings 1,2, and 3. 3rd fret

The Fm shape on Gm: Strings 1,2, and 3. 3rd fret

Try this:

The D7 shape is very useful all over the neck, as we have seen. Moving the D7 shape across the neck (on the first fret) , gives you D7, E6 or C#m, B7, and F#7.

{Note: The E6 could also be called C#m= C# E G#.

E6 = E G# (B) C#. The 5th is missing.}

Move the shapes randomly around the neck and name the chord as quickly as possible.

Chapter 19

The Pentatonic Scale

In Gm pentatonic we have G B♭C D F. **We can only create two chords from this scale: Gm and B♭**

Use the Gm and B♭ shapes you have learned to create more melodic lines in solos. Here are two chords to start with, you should know the rest. *If you don't know the other inversions, you need to review them. This is <u>VERY</u> important that you know them all over the neck!*

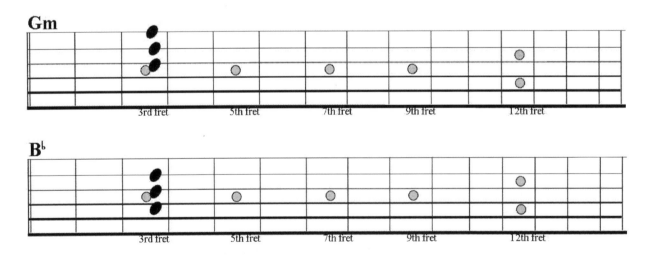

Chapter 20

Working with Modes

The modes, or "church modes," have been a focal point for guitar players for years. A mode is a scale.

This is an exciting part of the Guitar Apophenia process. If you are perhaps mystified by the modes, this will help. It is easy to understand the modes as a series of scales. Each scale or mode starts on the consecutive notes of a scale. In the key of C (no sharps or flats),

CDEFGABC   Ionian – the same as a major scale.

DEFGABCD   Dorian

EFGABCDE   Phrygian

FGABCDEF   Lydian

GABCDEFG   Mixolydian

ABCDEFG   Aeolian- the same as a minor scale.

BCDEFGAB   Locrian

 These are the modes. Notice that they are all parts of a C major scale. As you can see, each has it's own name. The difference between these is where the half steps occur in each mode. Each one is different.

My goal is to make this as easy to "hear", and understand as possible.

A shortcut to understanding modes is how to use them in a **parallel way**. Parallel= **that which is similar. Think of a train track with parallel rails. They are the same, but in different places.**

Make notes for anything you may need in this section for comparison! This is important!

Playing Modally:

  I just think of playing a scale from a different key over a chord. This is modal tonality. I struggled with the concept of parallel modes until I realized that they were major and minor scales from other keys. I already knew those scales! Rather than learn all of the modal scale patterns, I played the scales I knew. **The only difference was the target tones.** Rather than thinking that one particular mode has a flatted 3rd and 7th, I was simply playing a major scale. *This is where I could cause some controversy. Many guitar players will say you have to know the modal patterns starting on the root. My reply is that I don't always start my solo on the root. Learn one or two patterns from the root and you will be fine if you know the major and minor scales. I play thinking of several of the chords in the scale to give me unique note choices.*

  I identified and memorized where these modal scales were in relation to the key I was playing in. This is what I will show you now.

These are the modes for A with the first chord triads. The actual scales are underlined.

A	B	C#	D	E	F#	G#	A	Ionian	**A major**	Triad: A
A	B	C	D	E	F#	G	A	Dorian	**G major**	Triad: Am
A	B♭	C	D	E	F	G	A	Phrygian	**F major**	Triad: Am
A	B	C#	D#	E	F#	G#	A	Lydian	**E major**	Triad: A
A	B	C#	D	E	F#	G	A	Mixolydian	**D major**	Triad: A
A	B	C	D	E	F	G	A	Aeolian	**A minor**	Triad: Am
A	B♭	C	D	E♭	F	G	A	Locrian	**B♭ major**	Triad: A°

The underlined scales above are called the **"parent scales."**

Notice the minor and major modes designated by the root triad. The minor modes are played over an Am chord.

An easy way to memorize these:

Play an Am barre chord.

Dorian mode scale is down one step from your key. (G major)

Phyrgian is down two steps. (F major)

Now play an A barre chord.

Lydian is up a fifth- think power chord. (E major)

Mixolydian is up a fourth-straight across 6th string to 5th string.(D major)

Aeolian is in the same place. Am is called the parallel minor of A major. This would be played over Am.

Locrian- don't worry about it. It is unstable. The B° is a leading tone chord. It always wants to resolve and not good for a tonal center. This mode is not used very often. However, if you want to be a jazz major, learn everything.

Another thing to remember when improvising : You may also use the relative major (or minor) of each of these modes. That gives you more "ammunition". The *sound of the chord* makes the mode sound the way it is perceived by the listener.

We are switching keys to help you with remembering harmony.

Let's create the chords we can use playing G Dorian. Remember these chords are used here for improvisation ideas. Here again, use your ear. G major on the left, G Dorian on the right (F major)

I will do this as a comparison using G and Dorian (F). Creating chords:

G B D = G	I	**G B$^\flat$ D = Gm**	i	← Dorian
A C E = Am	ii	A C E = Am	ii	
B D F$^\sharp$ = Bm	iii	**B$^\flat$ D F = B$^\flat$**	**III**	
C E G = C	IV	C E G = C	IV	
D F$^\sharp$ A = D	V	D F A = Dm	v	
E G B = Em	vi	**E G B$^\flat$ = E$^{\circ}$**	**vi$^{\circ}$**	
F$^\sharp$ A C = F$^{\sharp\circ}$	vii$^{\circ}$	F A C = F	VII	

The B$^\flat$ and F natural are the "unique" tones. B$^\flat$ is a minor 3rd and F is the minor 7th.

You may notice that **Dorian is very similar to Gm pentatonic** (G B$^\flat$ C D F) that's why it works. <u>Dorian is used for songs in Gm</u> very frequently, as it is similar to Gm pentatonic. You may find that you like this tonality, rather than playing against G major. Playing over G major "forces" a 7 +9 tonality, common in blues. Think Hendrix.

Write out the chords in G minor now and compare them to F.

<u>Use the chord shapes you have learned to create melodic solos.</u>

Part B: Mixloxdian Mode

We will be playing against a G chord. Base this around a 12 Bar Blues, I, IV, V also. G major on the left, mixolydian on the right.

The parallel use of Mixloxdian is playing a C scale against the G.

G: G B D = G	G B D =G	or GBDF= G7
A C E = Am	A C E = Am	
B D F$^\sharp$ = Bm	**B D F = B^o**	or BDFA= B-7-5 *
C E G = C	C E G = C	
D F$^\sharp$ A = D	**D F A = Dm**	
E G B = Em	E G B = Em	
F$^\sharp$ A C = F$^{\sharp o}$	**F A C = F**	

The F natural is the "unique" tone; it's the minor 7th. Playing the notes of the C scale (starting on G) has the tonality of G7. This is great for rock, blues, and jazz. To play Mixloxdian, think of the major scale a fourth above the key you are playing. Visualization of the C being directly across from the G on the neck (up a 4th). Another point to remember: It is very common for players to change modes for each chord.

Use your ear! I can't stress that enough. Try playing Cmaj7 and Fmaj7 with a G chord. A great tonality of mixolydian!

*Good substitution for G9 is B-7-5, the upper chord tones.

Part C : Lydian Mode

We will be playing in G. Again, a 12 bar blues progression. **The parallel use of Lydian is playing a D scale over G.** We discussed this briefly before, but now we see the chords.

G B D = G	G B D = G
A C E = Am	**A C$^\sharp$ E = A major**
B D F$^\sharp$ = Bm	B D F$^\sharp$ = Bm
C E G = C	**C$^\sharp$ E G = C$^{\sharp\text{o}}$** ← Lydian
D F$^\sharp$ A = D	D F$^\sharp$ A = D
E G B = Em	E G B = Em
F$^\sharp$ A C = F$^{\sharp\text{o}}$	**F$^\sharp$ A C$^\sharp$ = F$^\sharp$m**

The "unique" tone here is the C$^\sharp$. This is a flat 5 or the "blue note" in the blues scale, also called $^\sharp$11.

You will notice that this scale is sounding a bit more "outside". It also sounds a bit more outside than the G Blues scale that contains the same C$^\sharp$/D$^\flat$ note. This is because the G Blues scale contains a F natural. (G B$^\flat$ C D$^\flat$ D F), the D$^\flat$ (C$^\sharp$) is the Blue note.

In Lydian, the presence of the F$^\sharp$ and the C$^\sharp$ together form a perfect 5th rather than the diminished 5th present in the G scale.

This accounts for part of the tonality of this scale. If we were play an A7 arpeggio over the G chord, we end up on G and we have also used the blue note.

A brief note on Phrygian: The third mode of C major is E Phrygian which is: E F G A B C D E. This is excellent to play over a Em chord. It gives the tonality of a flat 9 chord. An F natural rather than an F#.

Another common usage is Phrygian Dominant which is E F G#A B C D E. This creates the tonality of an E7-9 chord. This scale is an A harmonic minor scale, except you may wish to begin the scale on an E (the dominant, or five of A). It sounds great played against E7.You can research Phrygian Dominant more if you wish. It is a harmonic minor mode with a # 3. It is listed on the next page.

Write out the chords for Phrygian and Phrygian Dominant.

You many continue to do the other modes as we have done here. There are many more modes which are altered modes. There are also many ethnic scales from different regions of the world.

You will notice the tonality becoming increasingly "different" in ethnic scales. The familiarity of the tonal sound of each mode and scale is good for ear training.

Use the chord shapes you have learned to help create more melodic ideas in your solos.

Gradual Study:

Here is a list of the modes in C again. I have included the modes of the harmonic and melodic minor. Although I am not instructing on all of these, they are here for your resource. ***What are the parent scales?***

C Lydian	1♯ C D E F♯ G A B C
C Ionian (major)	C D E F G A B C
C Mixolydian	1♭ C D E F G A B♭ C
C Dorian	2♭ C D E♭ F G A B♭ C
C Aeolian (natural minor)	3♭ C D E♭ F G A♭ B♭ C
C Phrygian	4♭ C D♭ E♭ F G A♭ B♭ C
C Locrian	5♭ C D♭ E♭ F G♭ A♭ B♭ C

Harmonic Modes:

1.)Aeolian #7 - A B C D E F G# - AmMaj7(b6)
2) Locrian #6 - B C D E F G# A - Bm7b5/Bdim7
3) Ionian #5 - C D E F G# A B - Cmaj7#5
4) Dorian #4 - D E F G# A B C - Dm7(#11)
5) Phrygian #3 - E F G# A B C D - E7(b9,b13)
6) Lydian #2 - F G# A B C D E - Fmaj7(#9)
7) Mixolydian #1 - G# A B C D E F - G#dim7

Melodic Modes

1) **Dorian #7 - C D Eb F G A B - CmMaj7**
2) **Phrygian #6 - D Eb F G A B C - D7sus(b9)**
3) **Lydian #5 - Eb F G A B C D - Ebmaj7(#5)**
4) **Mixolydian #4 - F G A B C D Eb - F7(#11)**
5) **Aeolian #3 - G A B C D Eb F - G7(b13)**
6) **Locrian #2 - A B C D Eb F G - Am7b5(#9)**
7) **Ionian #1 - B C D Eb F G A - B7alt**

Pronunciation of modes: (So we don't appear stupid to our friends!)

Ionian- i Own ee an

Dorian- Door ee an

Phrygian- frah Gee an

Lydian- Lid ee an

Mixolydian- mixo Lid ee an

Aeolian- A ol ee an

Locrian- Low cree an

You may want to research more modal scales from a jazz theory book if you are interested in jazz. They will go more into detail of what mode goes with specific chords.

Chapter 21

A Look At More Chord Shapes

I have stayed within diatonic parameters throughout most of this book. You should find it easier to add altered tones with the knowledge that you have now.

I would like to give you a few more shapes to visualize that make a nice addition to playing.

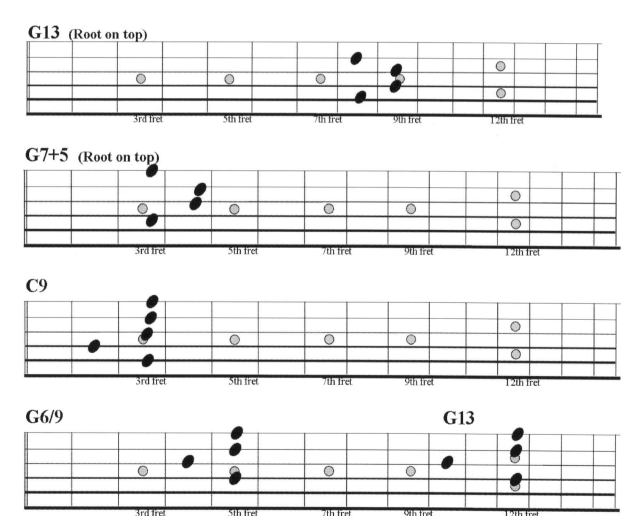

G13

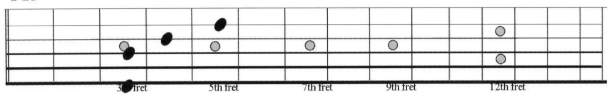

G13

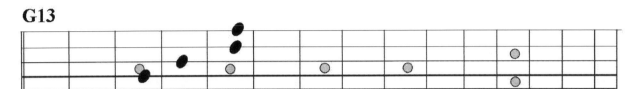

Space for notes

Closing

There are thousands of chords on the fretboard. You have a strong start, and now, the background to continue discovering more.

I suggest as a goal, learn one new thing every day. You will be surprised how easily this can be done. You should try to learn to play <u>every</u> chord in several places on the neck. The more you know, the more valued you will be among your peers.

We all have the same fret boards. Now we just "see it" in a different way.

Thank you and best of luck!

Ric Criste

You may contact me at <u>guitarapophenia@gmail.com</u>

Skype lessons are available. Contact me through the email.

A very special thanks to my family, friends, band mates, and the many students who gave me the inspiration for this project. Exceptional gratitude to Bill Miller, Jessalyn Stoltz, and Robert Lynn who helped me to finally get this into print. Many thanks to John Evanko for the tremendous cover art. Thanks to Garth Webber for ongoing inspiration. Thanks and love to my Julie for being by my side with all your support. To my dearest friend Nikita who taught me more about patience than anyone. To Anthony Resta, Jane, Barbara and Joe Resta - you are so dear to my heart, and you are my family.

This book is dedicated to my teachers: Edward McGuire, Annette Zalanowski, and my late dearest mother Shirley . I was blessed to have shared the opportunity to be with them in such a incredible learning experience.

48730416R00059

Made in the USA
Lexington, KY
11 January 2016